Who Named Their Pony MACARONI?

Poems about White House Pets

By Marilyn Singer ◆ Illustrations by Ryan McAmis

𝒟ISNEY · HYPERION

Los Angeles   New York

To Nancy, Martin, and Kathleen for all the Games Day fun —M.S.

For my dog, Bocce —R.M.

Acknowledgments: Thanks to Steve Aronson, Brenda Bowen, David Clark (trumanlibrary.org), Stacy Cordery (stacycordery.com), Becky Dalzell (rebeccadalzell.com), the Education Team at White House History (whitehousehistory.org), Spencer Howard (hoover.library@nara.gov), Kate Kelly (americacomesalive.com), Christopher Kenney (mckinleymuseum.org), Adam Lindquist (teddyrooseveltlive.com), Nancy Stetz (highland.org), and to my fabulous editors, Rotem Moscovich and Heather Crowley, and all the other wonderful folks at Disney • Hyperion.

First Edition, October 2019
10 9 8 7 6 5 4 3 2 1
FAC-029191-19235
Printed in Malaysia

This book is set in 14-point Perrywood/Monotype
Designed by Trish Parcell

Library of Congress Cataloging-in-Publication Data
Names: Singer, Marilyn, author. • McAmis, Ryan, illustrator.
Title: Who named their pony Macaroni? : poems about White House pets /
by Marilyn Singer ; illustrated by Ryan McAmis.
Description: First edition. • Los Angeles ; New York : Disney Hyperion,
2019.
Identifiers: LCCN 2018053228 • ISBN 9781484789995 (hardcover) • ISBN 1484789997 (hardcover)
Subjects: LCSH: Presidents' pets—United States—Juvenile poetry. • Children's poetry, American.
Classification: LCC PS3569.I546 W46 2019 • DDC 811/.54—dc23
LC record available at https://lccn.loc.gov/2018053228
Reinforced binding
Visit www.DisneyBooks.com

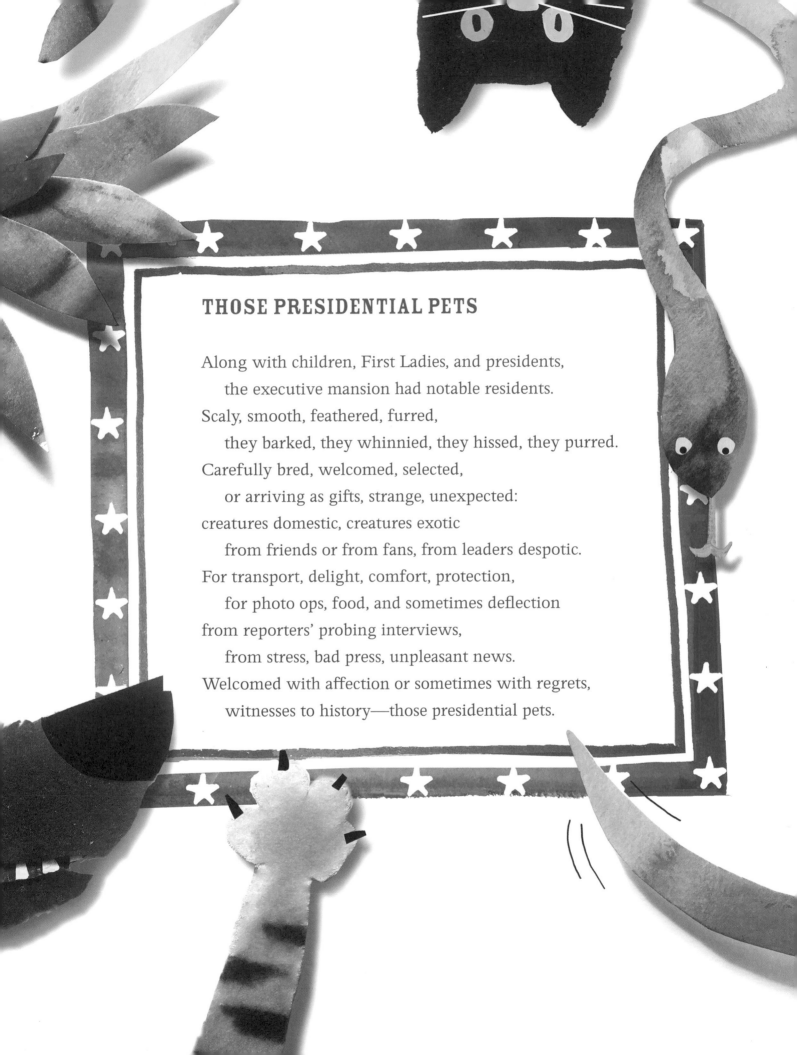

THOSE PRESIDENTIAL PETS

Along with children, First Ladies, and presidents,
   the executive mansion had notable residents.
Scaly, smooth, feathered, furred,
   they barked, they whinnied, they hissed, they purred.
Carefully bred, welcomed, selected,
   or arriving as gifts, strange, unexpected:
creatures domestic, creatures exotic
   from friends or from fans, from leaders despotic.
For transport, delight, comfort, protection,
   for photo ops, food, and sometimes deflection
from reporters' probing interviews,
   from stress, bad press, unpleasant news.
Welcomed with affection or sometimes with regrets,
   witnesses to history—those presidential pets.

GEORGE WASHINGTON'S DOGS

Besides having a country to lead,
he created a new dog breed,
known for its zest and its speed
(as well as its howling sound):
an American fox-hunting hound.

The mansion, plantation were rife
with canines throughout George's life
(he bought one or two for his wife).
Some were fierce, some frisky, some tame.
He gave every one a choice name.

Madame Moose was an elegant belle.
There were Sweetlips and Truelove as well.
Bold Vulcan stole food, so they tell.
To George, they were all of them jewels.
(Oh—and he also bred mules.)

9

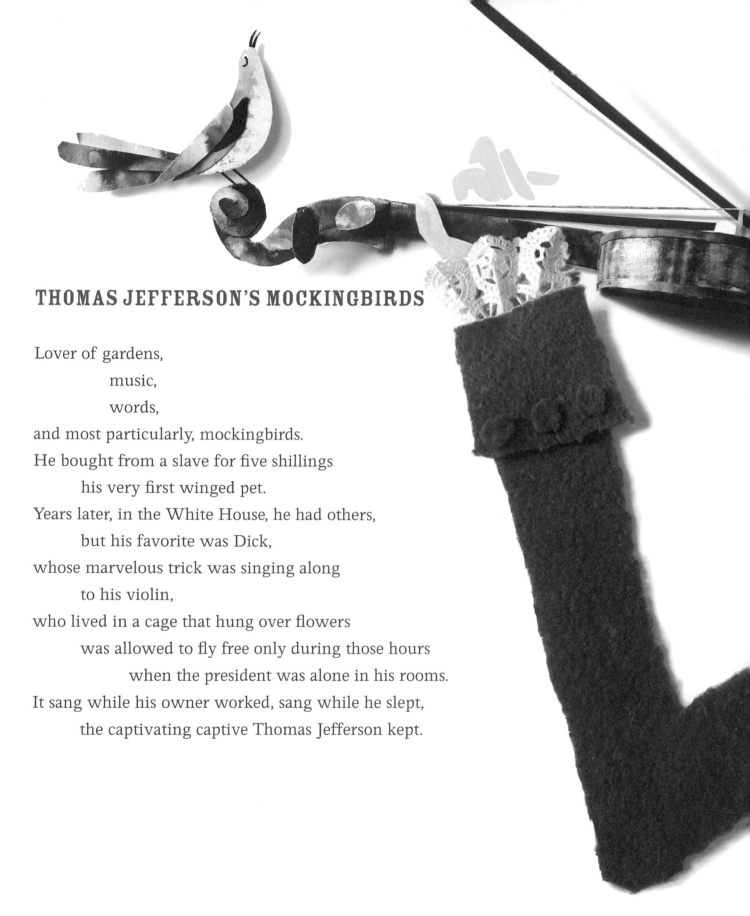

THOMAS JEFFERSON'S MOCKINGBIRDS

Lover of gardens,
      music,
      words,
and most particularly, mockingbirds.
He bought from a slave for five shillings
     his very first winged pet.
Years later, in the White House, he had others,
     but his favorite was Dick,
whose marvelous trick was singing along
     to his violin,
who lived in a cage that hung over flowers
     was allowed to fly free only during those hours
        when the president was alone in his rooms.
It sang while his owner worked, sang while he slept,
     the captivating captive Thomas Jefferson kept.

THE ADAMS SILKWORMS

Perhaps you would not call them pets,
   the silkworms John Quincy's wife, Louisa, raised.
After all, they were not her constant companions,
Nor did she give them names.

But as her husband watched her
   patiently winding their silk for her sewing,
did he note how they gave her a kind of comfort?
Did he feel a touch of envy that,
   just for the moment,
she was not thinking about the turbulent world
   of politics?

UNUSUAL PETS

John Quincy Adams received an alligator
    from the Marquis de Lafayette.
He most likely did not choose it.
But how could he refuse it?

Van Buren took delight in his two tiger cubs
    from the Sultan of Oman.
Though he wanted to keep them, it's true,
they went to a local zoo.

Buchanan was offered some elephants
    by the generous King of Siam.
But it was Lincoln who found that absurd,
and tactfully turned down the herd.

A president must be a diplomat
    and tender most careful regrets
when declining unusual creatures
    that do not make marvelous pets.

ANDREW JACKSON'S PARROT

He bought his wife a parrot, named it Poll.
He thought it would bring his dear Rachel joy.
The bird was destined to outlive them all
and find unusual ways to annoy.
When Jackson died with long forewarning,
the parrot proved she was rather perverse.
At his funeral, while folks were mourning,
she flapped and she squawked, then began to curse.
Was it at banks or at rivals' supporters?
At the wealthy elite, at the V.P.?
At fellow lawyers, disliked reporters?
At the Seminole, Creek, or Cherokee?
Who could have taught Poll such scandalous words?
(A hint: It surely was *not* other birds.)

ZACHARY TAYLOR'S OLD WHITEY

He was a warhorse, never afraid.
    He shone with Rough and Ready pride.
Happy to prance in any parade,
    he was a warhorse, never afraid.
His reputation didn't fade,
    even when his master died.
He was a warhorse, never afraid.
    He shone with Rough and Ready pride.

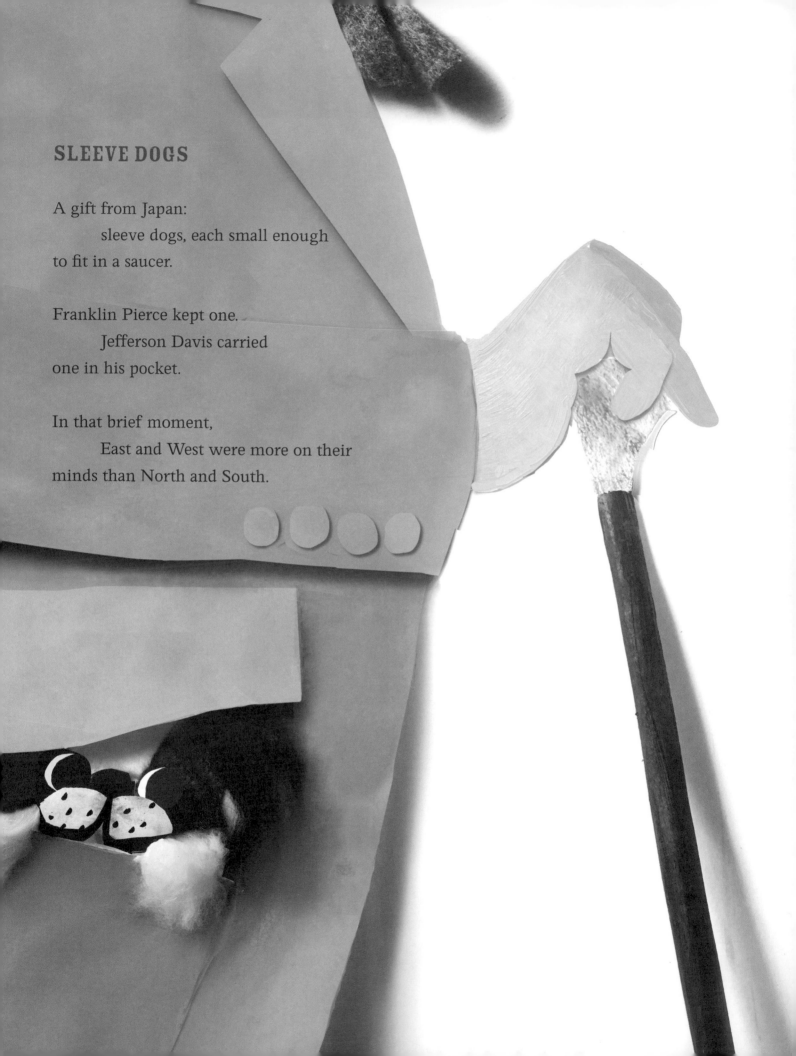

SLEEVE DOGS

A gift from Japan:
     sleeve dogs, each small enough
to fit in a saucer.

Franklin Pierce kept one.
     Jefferson Davis carried
one in his pocket.

In that brief moment,
     East and West were more on their
minds than North and South.

JAMES BUCHANAN'S BALD EAGLES

The bald eagle, majestic, mighty.
A strong flier, but not flighty.
Our country's symbol, our figurehead,
admired (also hunted,
      killed by pesticides and lead).
Emblem of freedom, a bird not designed
      to be a pet, to be confined.
So what was on Buchanan's mind
      to keep a caged pair?
Did he study them and hope to share
      their power to become
      (and this is speculative)
a respected and forceful chief executive?
If so, it was to no avail:
That president was doomed to fail.

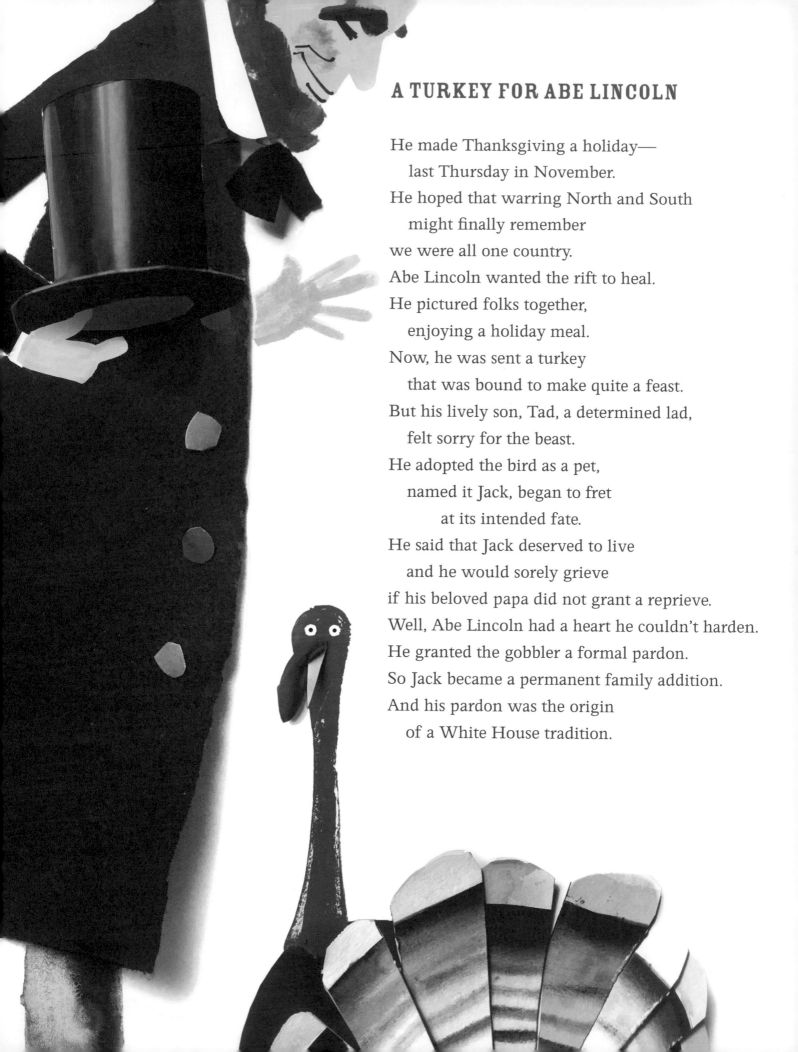

A TURKEY FOR ABE LINCOLN

He made Thanksgiving a holiday—
    last Thursday in November.
He hoped that warring North and South
    might finally remember
we were all one country.
Abe Lincoln wanted the rift to heal.
He pictured folks together,
    enjoying a holiday meal.
Now, he was sent a turkey
    that was bound to make quite a feast.
But his lively son, Tad, a determined lad,
    felt sorry for the beast.
He adopted the bird as a pet,
    named it Jack, began to fret
        at its intended fate.
He said that Jack deserved to live
    and he would sorely grieve
if his beloved papa did not grant a reprieve.
Well, Abe Lincoln had a heart he couldn't harden.
He granted the gobbler a formal pardon.
So Jack became a permanent family addition.
And his pardon was the origin
    of a White House tradition.

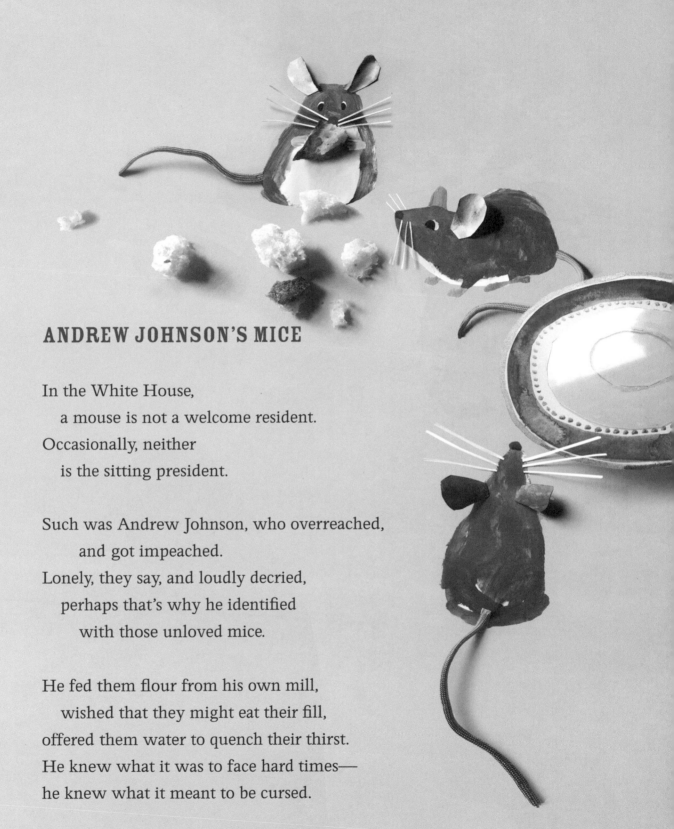

ANDREW JOHNSON'S MICE

In the White House,
   a mouse is not a welcome resident.
Occasionally, neither
   is the sitting president.

Such was Andrew Johnson, who overreached,
   and got impeached.
Lonely, they say, and loudly decried,
   perhaps that's why he identified
     with those unloved mice.

He fed them flour from his own mill,
   wished that they might eat their fill,
offered them water to quench their thirst.
He knew what it was to face hard times—
he knew what it meant to be cursed.

Tried by the Senate and then acquitted,
   he finished out his term.
What happened to his rodent friends,
   no one can confirm.

THERE WAS NO HORSE GRANT COULDN'T RIDE

There was no horse Grant couldn't ride.
There was no horse he couldn't tame.
He prized each steed he sat astride.

In horsemanship he took great pride.
At West Point this talent made him a name.
There was no horse Grant couldn't ride.

Some mounts were calm and dignified.
Some thought that battles were a game.
He prized each steed he sat astride.

Some were lost and others died.
Some lived on to great acclaim.
There was no horse Grant couldn't ride.

He claimed a Southern pony and then felt justified
in giving it rebel Jeff Davis's name.
He prized each steed he sat astride.

Cincinnati, a charger, helped preside
at Appomattox, of war's-end fame.
There was no horse Grant couldn't ride.

As general, Grant was glorified.
As president, not . . . but just the same,
there was no horse Grant couldn't ride.
He prized each steed he sat astride.

THE HAYES FAMILY'S CAT

Perhaps
her ancestors
dwelled in palaces with kings.
But Siam was at home in the
White House.

She lived
a life too brief,
but her charm and her fame
were such, folks took to these felines
so much

that soon
throughout our land,
Siamese cats were found
in lodgings considerably
less grand.

JAMES GARFIELD'S VETO

He named his dog Veto, with a wicked wink
    at a contrary Congress, to make them think:
A bill to sign? Why, I might refuse it.
    The power was his (though he'd never get to use it).

Veto was a hero, saved his family from harm.
    When the barn caught fire, he barked out an alarm.
Once, with brains and determined force
    he clung to the reins of a rampaging horse.

That Newfoundland might have prevented disaster
    if only he'd been with his ill-fated master
on that terrible day when James Garfield was shot.
But as everyone knows, alas, he was not.

16

OLD WHISKERS, THE WHITE HOUSE GOAT

Imagine a gentleman running
    in a top hat and long frock coat,
hollering, "Stop!" and waving his cane
    at a runaway billy goat
that was pulling a cart with his grandchild inside.
It's a picture without comparison!
Imagine how people might have laughed
    at their president, Benjamin Harrison,
a man thought cool and dignified,
    not prone to unflattering capers.
No wonder it took about ten years
    for the story to get in the papers.

NAME GAME

To know history well it may be critical
to view some pets' names as political.

Ben Harrison's possums were called with affection,
Mr. Reciprocity and Mr. Protection,
for the Republican policy on tariffs and trade.
Folks might have liked the possums,
but thought Ben had overstayed.

The Civil War was a fight he didn't want to hasten,
but Millard Fillmore named his ponies, Dixon and Mason,
for the line between slave states and ones that were free.
And he signed into law pro-Southern policy.

Budget Bureau and Tax Reduction, lion cubs,
were owned by Calvin Coolidge, responsible for flubs
that helped lead to times of boom, then bust—
too many Americans left in the dust.

Yet whether they failed or succeeded,
one thing presidents have always needed—
and this is true; it's not a rumor:
they had to keep their sense of humor.

TR'S MENAGERIE

Tusks and elephant feet,
   hat racks made of antlers,
   mountain lion rugs,
   butterflies and other bugs:
      trophies and specimens,
      in museums, in his home.
Hunting was sport, self-reliance,
   natural science.

But he liked them alive, too:
      hyena, macaw, flying squirrel,
      badger, bear, barn owl,
      numerous fowl, two kangaroo rats,
      horses, dogs, feisty cats.
Each one a pet.

Though it may be hard to understand,
   Theodore Roosevelt loved this land—
      its features, its creatures.
How he wanted them conserved, preserved.
How he loved the untamed.
Perhaps the White House was a place he
   couldn't abide
unless he brought the wild inside.

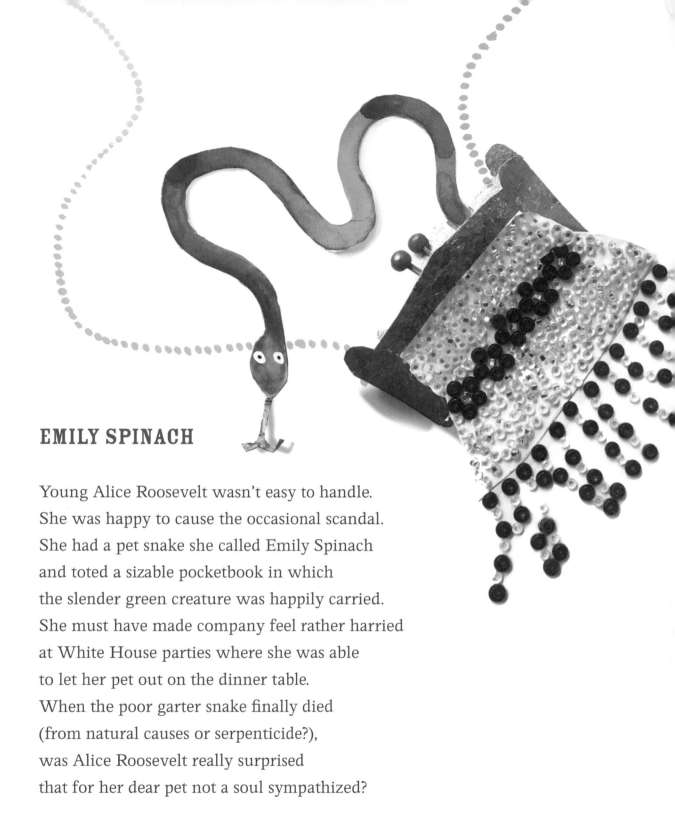

EMILY SPINACH

Young Alice Roosevelt wasn't easy to handle.
She was happy to cause the occasional scandal.
She had a pet snake she called Emily Spinach
and toted a sizable pocketbook in which
the slender green creature was happily carried.
She must have made company feel rather harried
at White House parties where she was able
to let her pet out on the dinner table.
When the poor garter snake finally died
(from natural causes or serpenticide?),
was Alice Roosevelt really surprised
that for her dear pet not a soul sympathized?

PAULINE WAYNE

Once there were cows at the White House.
      How else to get butter and milk?
For decades they grazed on the grass there.
      Pauline Wayne was the last of her ilk.

Featured in all the newspapers,
      this bovine, productive and prized,
was pastured when Taft's term was over—
      and milk had to be pasteurized.

THE WILSONS' SHEEP

The idea was sheep—
   to keep the White House lawns cheaply trimmed,
   to sell their fleece to support the Red Cross.
So agreed Mr. Wilson, our country's boss.
Heading the flock was a ram named Old Ike,
   ornery, smart, a bit of a wacko,
who liked to charge and chew tobacco.

But it was all for the good of a country at war:
Indoors there were no-meat, no-wheat, and no-heat days
   (no festive dinners, no soirees).
So declared Mrs. Wilson, our country's First Lady.

It was:
   economize, donate,
   pull your own weight.
By 1920, the sheep numbered 48.
They ate up the backyard
   and were working on the front.
The war was long since over.
They were causing too much harm.
It was time to ship them off
   to do their dining on a farm.

REBECCA RACCOON AND COMPANY

When you live on a farm
and are quite shy,
    which Calvin Coolidge was,
you may grow up to be a guy
who likes beings with feathers and fuzz
        more than folks.
Then when you are president,
        your penchant provokes
        people to send you critters, domestic, exotic,
turning your household into something chaotic.
Pets that aren't pets, with which you can't cope:
        black bear, wallaby,
        pygmy hippo, antelope.
Also a raccoon . . .
Now, this isn't a tall tale, a lie, or a fable:
That creature was sent for the Thanksgiving table.
But just like Lincoln's turkey, Jack,
Rebecca (so they named her) did not become a snack.
Cal and his wife, Grace, made her a special friend
        (one we would not recommend).
She posed for famous photographs,
was prone to making maddening gaffes:
clawing at furniture, ripping people's clothes
(in particular, expensive silk hose).
She'd sit on Cal's lap by the fireplace—
and escape any cage to lead a wild chase.
She had to go.
And so they sent her (like those others) to the zoo.
The White House staff thought, *Whew! Good Golly,*
next time perhaps they will stick with a collie.

FDR'S FALA

From Laddie Boy to Rob Roy
    straight on through to Bo,
a canine's job has been to show
    that our nation's chief is just an average Joe,
to prove that our leader isn't cold or snotty.
Perhaps most famous of the pack
    was Fala, Roosevelt's Scottie,
who accompanied the president on many trips
    by trains and planes and battleships
from Mexico to Newfoundland.
Who witnessed history being made firsthand.
An honorary private, he raised funds to fight a war,
    starred in a short movie, got fan mail galore.
Now cast in bronze, he remains
the sole First Dog to be
    memorialized with his master
in Washington, D.C.

FELLER

Didn't want, didn't need, that cocker spaniel pup
    someone gave him as a gift,
so Harry Truman gave him up
    to his personal physician,
    angered folks with his decision.
The dog's stay with the doctor
        turned out to be brief.
Next, he lived at Camp David,
    'til to everyone's relief,
he went off to a farm in Ohio
        to live out his days happily.
As for Harry Truman, he lived out *his* pet-free.

PUSHINKA

Pushinka,
       daughter of the first dog
to orbit the earth and survive—
a charming gift from Khrushchev to JFK.
A gesture of will and goodwill:
       that Russia was leading the race to space,
       that Russia's heart was in the right place.
Even amid such fierce rivalry,
       real warmth wasn't lost.
Some think that fluffy dog helped prevent the cost
       of nuclear destruction,
believe it or not,
       by checking the Cold War
          from becoming all too Hot.

MACARONI

There's a photo of JFK's daughter
        on the horse her parents bought her—
           a sturdy little pony.
They called it Macaroni
        from the well-known song (although in that
           it really meant the Yankee's hat).
Neil Diamond, who found the picture winning,
        wrote a tune sung every eighth inning
           at Boston's Fenway Park.
Fans join in for a lark.
They all know every line.
        So good . . ."Sweet Caroline"!

LYNDON BAINES JOHNSON LOVED HIS DOGS

LBJ loved his dogs,
      thought everyone should know it.
On several occasions,
      he chose odd ways to show it.

Reporters watched him pull up Him,
      the beagle, by his ears.
Folks did not approve at all—
      the act was met with jeers—
so he was told it would be wise
      to tell them, "I apologize."

In front of an ambassador,
      he offered no regrets,
when he and his mutt, Yuki,
      howled out duets.
Nor did he think it was uncool
      for them to share the White House pool.

Yet when he wanted Yuki
      in his daughter's wedding photo,
his wife, Lady Bird, declared it was absurd—
      most certainly a no-no.
Perhaps she spoiled his fun,
      but in the end, she won.

On several occasions,
      though, he chose odd ways to show it.
It's clear that Lyndon loved his dogs,
      and thought the world should know it.

CHECKERS

It's a curious fact:
A dog can make
 a president.
Years before he won the White House,
  accused of being bribed with secret donations,
  his career nearly wrecked,
Richard Nixon went on TV and made a speech.
He was firm, didn't squirm. He didn't beseech.
He admitted to one gift that he vowed to keep:
  Checkers, the spaniel his daughters adored.
Nixon scored.
A victorious vice president he became,
  then went on to greater fame
   (and later, disgrace).
By then, the dog was gone.
Yet Checkers's name lives on.
A synonym for Nixon's strategy,
  emotional, savvy, and sly,
A dog who made a president,
  though he couldn't have known how he did it,
  nor could he have known why.

REX THE GHOSTBUSTER

Ronald Reagan liked to boast
that Rex, his dog, had seen a ghost—
Honest Abe, to be exact,
though none confirmed it as a fact.
But it was him we must presume
since Rex went nuts outside the room
where Lincoln was once known to sit.
The spaniel also had a fit
at something no one else could see
where the Reagans watched TV.
Things we know that aren't bunk:
This dog had a lot of spunk,
got a tonsillectomy,
lit the White House Christmas tree.
But was the dog a real ghostbuster,
or was that all a lot of bluster?

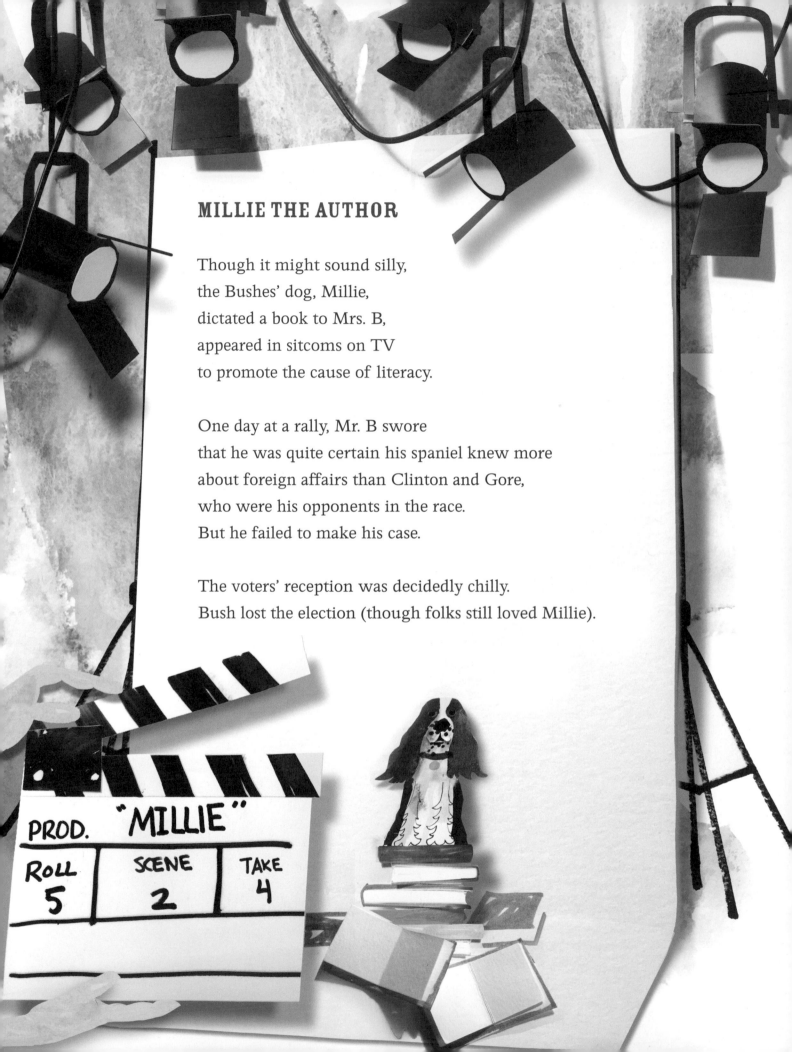

MILLIE THE AUTHOR

Though it might sound silly,
the Bushes' dog, Millie,
dictated a book to Mrs. B,
appeared in sitcoms on TV
to promote the cause of literacy.

One day at a rally, Mr. B swore
that he was quite certain his spaniel knew more
about foreign affairs than Clinton and Gore,
who were his opponents in the race.
But he failed to make his case.

The voters' reception was decidedly chilly.
Bush lost the election (though folks still loved Millie).

PROD. "MILLIE"

ROLL 5   SCENE 2   TAKE 4

BAD DOGGY, BAD KITTY

Even though they are first pets,
some are bound to misbehave.
But they rarely show regrets,
even though they are first pets.
Such demeanor quite upsets
the chief exec and his enclave.
Even though they are first pets,
some are bound to misbehave.

Some were hits and some were misses.
But even good pets have bad days.
Socks the Cat was prone to hisses.
Some were hits and some were misses.
Sunny knocked a girl down, then covered her with kisses
(she's likely learned to mend her ways).
Some were hits and some were misses.
But even good ones have bad days.

EPITAPHS AT THE WHITE HOUSE

Here lies the Eisenhower parakeet,
sweet from tail to beak.
His given name was Gabby,
but he didn't speak.

Robin the canary,
sunlight on the wing,
mourned by Caroline Kennedy.
How he loved to sing!

Two little graves,
were once dug here
for two little birds
some children held dear.

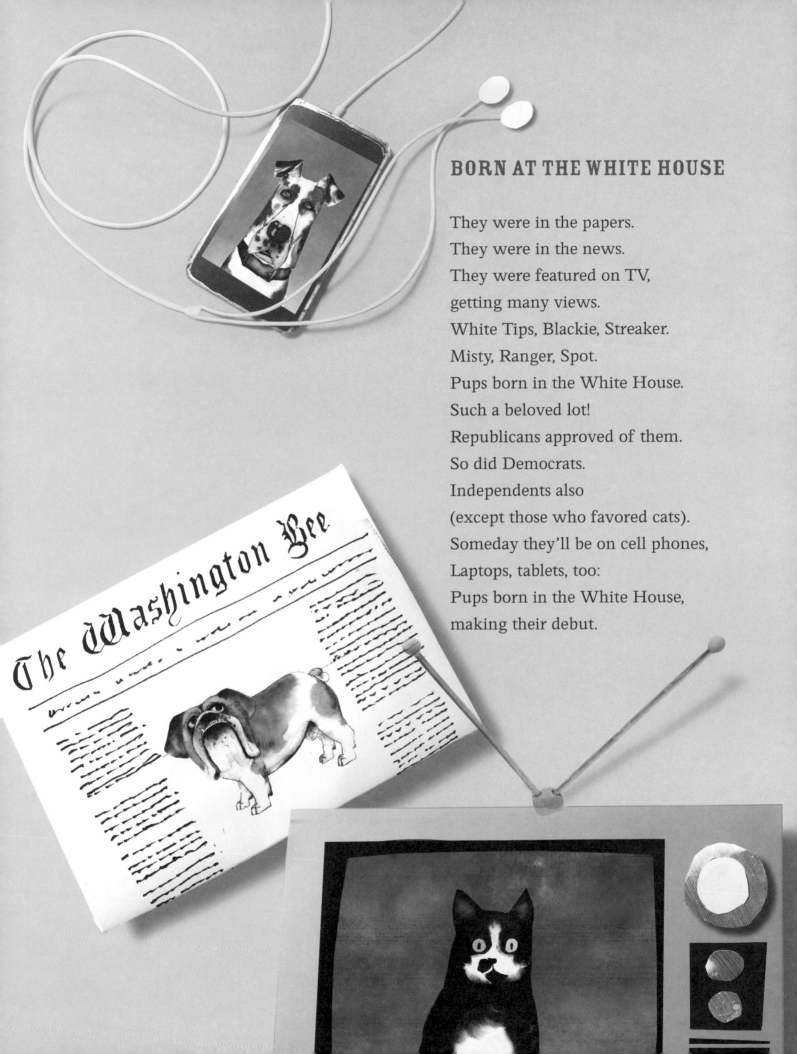

BORN AT THE WHITE HOUSE

They were in the papers.
They were in the news.
They were featured on TV,
getting many views.
White Tips, Blackie, Streaker.
Misty, Ranger, Spot.
Pups born in the White House.
Such a beloved lot!
Republicans approved of them.
So did Democrats.
Independents also
(except those who favored cats).
Someday they'll be on cell phones,
Laptops, tablets, too:
Pups born in the White House,
making their debut.

The Washington Bee

EXECUTIVE PETS

It's thought that **George Washington** owned as many as fifty canines during his lifetime. They included Madame Moose, a Dalmatian, and many spaniels, terriers, and hounds, which accompanied him when he went hunting. Besides being known as "the Father of Our Country," Washington is also called "the Father of the American Foxhound." He helped create the breed by crossing French hounds with his own black-and-tan hounds. He also bred mules. Washington had the first presidential pets, but none of them ever lived in the White House because neither did he. The executive mansion was not completed until John Adams became president.

During **John Adams**'s term in office, the White House stables were constructed, and they housed his carriage horses, Caesar and Cleopatra, as well as several others. He and his wife, Abigail Adams, liked giving their pets interesting names. They owned two mixed-breed dogs called Juno and Satan, the first canines to run on the White House lawn.

During his lifetime, **Thomas Jefferson** had several pet mockingbirds. In 1772, he purchased his first for five shillings from a slave, then added more to his household. Twelve years later, when he was minister to France, he even brought one along. His favorite bird, the only one mentioned by name in his journals, was Dick, who would sing when Jefferson played his violin. Dick would also fly around his office when the president was working there. The rest of the time, the bird stayed in his cage, hanging by the window amid the roses and geraniums. Margaret Bayard Smith, Jefferson's friend and an early historian, wrote, "How he loved the bird! He could not live without something to love."

James Madison didn't have any pets, but his wife, **Dolley**, did—a macaw named Polly. The First Lady would often greet guests with Polly perched on her shoulder. When the British burned the

White House during the War of 1812, Dolley saved a few items—George Washington's portrait, some important documents, and Polly. Parrots have long lives, and Polly outlived James Madison. It's possible she also outlasted Dolley, but no one is sure.

James Monroe presided during a period known as the Era of Good Feelings—a time of unity after the War of 1812. It's uncertain whether, like Madison before him, he had pets, though his daughter, Maria, did own a small black spaniel.

When the Marquis de Lafayette, the French general who was a hero of the American Revolution, toured the United States, he received many gifts. One of them was an alligator, which he gave to President **John Quincy Adams**. The reptile took up residence in the White House's East Room, where John Quincy liked to show it off to visitors. His wife, **Louisa**, kept rather different creatures at the executive mansion: silkworms. Louisa was in charge of raising them and harvesting the silk, which she used in her sewing. Some historians feel that the silkworm project was a means for her to deal with depression and boredom.

Andrew Jackson, aka "Old Hickory," loved horses—and horse racing. Before he became president, he was famed in Tennessee for breeding thoroughbreds. After his election, Jackson created a racing stable that could house ten horses or so on the White House grounds. Andrew bought an African gray parrot named Poll for his beloved wife, Rachel. Apparently, it picked up some of Old Hickory's rough language. At Jackson's funeral, Poll swore so much and so loudly that it had to be removed from the house. Reverend Norment, who led the service, described the attendees as being "horrified and awed at the bird's lack of reverence."

Presidents have been known to receive unusual presents, particularly from foreign dignitaries or heads of state. **Martin Van Buren** was given a pair of tiger cubs by the Sultan of Oman, and he was thrilled. He intended to keep the big cats at the White House. But Congress said no, insisting that they belonged to the American people and not the chief executive. Eventually, Van Buren was forced to give the tigers to a local zoo.

William Henry Harrison served the shortest term of any president. He died of pneumonia after one month in office. During his tenure, he kept a goat and a cow at the White House, which was not an uncommon practice. Both animals kept the grass trimmed and provided milk, butter, and cheese.

When Harrison died, his vice president, **John Tyler**, became chief executive. Like many other presidents, John Tyler liked dogs, but he especially prized his horses. When his favorite died, Tyler had the horse buried on his plantation with this epitaph: "Here lies the body of my good horse, 'The General.' For 20 years he bore me around the circuit of my practice, and in all that time he never made a blunder. Would that his master could say the same!"

Little known before his candidacy, **James K. Polk** believed in expanding the country and added a vast amount of territory to it. Although he, too, liked horses, he didn't keep any at the White House. In fact, there is no record of his having had any pets at all.

Nicknamed "Old Rough and Ready," **Zachary Taylor** was a war hero who loved his faithful steed, Old Whitey, as much as John Tyler adored The General. Old Whitey was a warhorse, who stayed calm and steady during many a battle of the Mexican-American War. The horse outlived Zachary, who died just sixteen months into his presidency. During the funeral procession, Old Whitey marched behind the wagon carrying the president's casket.

Millard Fillmore's ponies Mason and Dixon were named after the surveyors who drew the border between the Northern and Southern states. Fillmore was staunchly anti-slavery, but he tried to avoid a civil war by signing the Compromise of 1850. It was meant to appease both the North and the South, but it embittered the North by including the Fugitive Slave Act, which required that escaped slaves in all states be returned to their owners. After leaving office, he was a founder and vice president of the Buffalo chapter of the American Society for the Prevention of Cruelty to Animals (ASPCA).

A Northerner with pro-Southern sympathies, **Franklin Pierce** was not a well-regarded president. But he did succeed in opening trade relations with Japan, which had closed its borders nearly two hundred years before. Commodore Matthew Perry, the chief negotiator of the treaty, brought back gifts from the Japanese, including seven toy dogs, probably Japanese Chins. Because they could fit into the sleeves of a kimono, they were called "sleeve dogs." Franklin kept one canine and gave the others to friends, including then Secretary of War Jefferson Davis who went on to become president of the Confederacy.

James Buchanan tried and failed to appease both the North and the South, further dividing the country and ushering in the Civil War. Unmarried and without children, Buchanan brought his beloved Newfoundland dog, Lara, to Washington for companionship. While in office, James received as a gift two bald eagles, symbols of America since 1782. The birds did not fare well in the White House and were eventually sent to Buchanan's estate in Pennsylvania. King Mongkut of Siam wrote to Buchanan, offering some creatures even more unusual than the eagles—elephants.

But the king's letter did not reach James. Instead, it went to the next president, Abraham Lincoln, who turned down the offer.

Throughout his life, **Abraham Lincoln** showed a fondness for all animals. When he was a child, he tried—and failed—to save the family pig from slaughter. When he became president and his dog, Fido, proved to be too overwhelmed by the bustle of Washington, D.C., Lincoln found a good family to care for him. He even had Fido's favorite sofa sent to their home so the dog would be comfortable. His secretary of state, William Seward, gave him two kittens, which the president adored. Later, a variety of other creatures came to live at the White House. These included dogs, rabbits, goats, and ponies. And then there was a turkey named Jack. In late 1863, the bird was a gift intended to become Christmas dinner. But like his father before him, Tad Lincoln, age ten, decided that the animal shouldn't be killed. He succeeded where his dad failed, insisting that Abe sign an "order of reprieve." Years later, with George H. W. Bush, the presidential turkey pardon became a formal tradition at Thanksgiving, the celebration that Lincoln himself made an official American holiday in the hope of uniting the warring North and South.

After Lincoln's assassination, **Andrew Johnson** became president. When the Civil War ended, Congress passed a law saying that he couldn't fire any Cabinet members. Johnson tried to dismiss the secretary of war, so Congress impeached him—though it failed to remove him from office. During the impeachment process, Andrew hid out in his rooms, where he befriended a family of mice, leaving them food and drink. "The little fellows give me their confidence," he told his secretary, "and I give them their basket and pour upon the hearth some water that they might quench their thirst."

As a boy, **Ulysses S. Grant** was so small and quiet that schoolmates unkindly gave him the nickname "Useless." But even then it was clear that Grant excelled in the area of horsemanship. During the Civil War, as commander of the Union army, Ulysses rode several steeds. The most famous were Cincinnati, which he rode into battle, and Jeff Davis, a surefooted and unruly pony that was captured on a Southern plantation. Grant purchased the horse from the army and proceeded to tame him. When Ulysses became president, Cincinnati was one of the horses that pulled Grant's carriage. The president and his family owned other pets, including a Newfoundland named Faithful, but horses were most near and dear to the war hero's heart.

In 1877, the American Humane Society was formed. It was the same year that **Rutherford B. Hayes**, his family, and their many pets moved into the White House. A supporter of the AHS, Hayes addressed Congress on the subject in the hope that it would enact laws to prevent animal abuse. Rutherford owned dogs, birds, cows, and a goat, but his rarest animal was a Siamese cat. In

Siam (now called Thailand), this breed was owned by royalty. The American consul to Bangkok was able to acquire a cat as a gift for the president. Most likely the first Siamese in the U.S., Siam, as they called her, made quite a splash.

James Garfield's Newfie, Veto, was reportedly a genuine canine hero, saving the family on more than one occasion. The dog's master had a sense of humor. By naming him Veto, James was telling Congress that he might not approve all of its bills. Garfield was shot by a malcontented office-seeker just four months into his term, and he died two and a half months later.

Upon Garfield's death, **Chester A. Arthur** became president. He had a pair of perfectly matched horses to pull his carriage. He liked fine clothes, furniture, and decoration. The carriage was fancy, and the horses were described as "beautiful." Chester wouldn't have been satisfied with anything less.

Among their many pets, **Grover Cleveland** and his young wife, Frances, had a prize-winning St. Bernard, a popular poodle, and some of the first dachshunds to live in the U.S. The only president to serve two nonconsecutive terms, Cleveland also kept hundreds of decorative fish. These included paradise fish from Siam and Japanese goldfish, which swam in the White House conservatory pools.

The grandson of William Henry Harrison, **Benjamin Harrison** named his opossums Mr. Reciprocity and Mr. Protection, after his trade policy. When the U.S. went into a financial depression, Harrison was voted out, and Cleveland returned to office for his second, nonconsecutive term. Benjamin also had a goat, Old Whiskers, which pulled his grandchildren's cart. One day, the critter took off down Executive Avenue with a child in tow. Observers saw the president racing after the goat and finally catching him. Years later, the incident was reported in a newspaper: "It was an exciting race . . . and it looked for a time that the goat would be victorious. It also demonstrated that the former president of the United States was a sprinter of no mean ability."

William McKinley led the country through the Spanish-American War, made the U.S. a presence in Cuba, obtained Puerto Rico, Guam, and the Philippines, and annexed Hawaii. He had a parrot named Washington Post, possibly after the newspaper or after the march (a type of song) by John Philip Sousa. The bird was certainly musical. It was taught to whistle "Yankee Doodle Dandy." The president gave Washington Post the job of White House greeter. Unlike Andrew Jackson's parrot, Washington Post did not swear.

Theodore Roosevelt became president when McKinley was assassinated. He had poor health as a child, but he was determined to conquer that by learning to ride and jump horses. An avid hunter, he killed and mounted many specimens. He was equally fascinated with living creatures and kept a variety of domestic and exotic pets, some well-behaved, others not. His favorite dog, Pete, a bull terrier, had to be removed from the White House after tearing the French ambassador's pants. Josiah, a badger, was also a nipper and eventually went to a zoo, as did TR's lion, hyena, zebra, and at least one of his five bears. Other pets stayed. Kermit, one of Roosevelt's six children, liked to carry the kangaroo rats in his pockets. Ted Jr. was photographed with Eli Yale, a hyacinth macaw, on his shoulder. Then there was Alice's pet snake, Emily Spinach. Alice liked to carry the snake in her purse and occasionally lay it on the table at White House dinners. When asked why she gave the reptile its name, she replied that it was "as green as spinach and as thin as my Aunt Emily."

Like several previous presidents, **William Howard Taft** kept cows at the White House. Pauline Wayne was a gift from Senator Stephenson of Wisconsin. Miss Wayne, as she was called, provided milk, cheese, and butter for the First Family and was quite a star. At the International Dairymen's Exposition in Milwaukee in 1911, souvenir bottles of her milk sold for fifty cents apiece. On her way to the show, her train car was accidentally switched, and the cow disappeared for several days—to be rescued in the nick of time from a slaughterhouse. Toward the end of Taft's term, Miss Wayne's health declined and she was returned to Stephenson's farm. She was the last bovine to live at the executive mansion.

Woodrow Wilson tried and failed to keep the U.S. out of World War I. To help the war effort and cut costs, the White House installed a flock of sheep to trim the lawn. At auction, the wool sold for $52,823, an astounding sum in those days, and the money was donated to the Red Cross. The donation from the following year's wool went to the Salvation Army. Among the sheep was an ornery ram named Old Ike. He was fond of chewing tobacco, especially cigar butts. After a few years, Ike and the rest of the sheep were sent to a farm in Maryland.

The first celebrity dog covered by the press was **Warren G. Harding**'s Airedale, Laddie Boy. He had his portrait painted and sat in his own chair at Cabinet meetings. At his second birthday party, the canine was served a cake made of dog biscuits. First Lady Florence Harding took on animal abuse as an issue and featured Laddie at events to promote good care. When Harding died in office, as a memorial and tribute to the president's background as a newspaperman, newsboys collected 19,134 pennies that were melted down and sculpted into a statue of the famous dog.

Like the Roosevelts, **Calvin Coolidge** and his wife, Grace, had a menagerie of familiar and unusual creatures. Grace was especially fond of white collies. Her official portrait features one of them, Rob Roy. Calvin received gifts of wild animals, which he sent to a zoo, including a bobcat, a pygmy hippo known as Billy, and two lion cubs. As a reference to his policies of cutting taxes and reducing government spending, Coolidge called the cubs Tax Reduction and Budget Bureau. Another gift was a raccoon, which the sender thought would make a good Thanksgiving dinner. However, the Coolidges fell in love with the critter and named her Rebecca. The raccoon got a fancy collar and was photographed in the First Lady's arms. But Rebecca was trouble. She ripped upholstery and ladies' stockings, scratched people, and escaped cages. Fearing for the animal's safety, Grace sadly sent her to a zoo as well.

A dog helped **Herbert Hoover** get elected. He was viewed as stiff and serious and he needed something to make him seem more approachable. A photo of him and his Belgian shepherd, King Tut, did the trick. Unfortunately, King Tut did not fare well at the White House. He found it too stressful and refused to eat. Herbert did not fare well either. The prosperity of the Roaring Twenties gave way to the Great Depression. Hoover's response to the crisis was a failure. No dog could help him win a second term.

Although **Franklin Delano Roosevelt** had six other dogs, none were as famous as Fala. The Scottish terrier traveled everywhere with the president—from fishing trips to major conferences. World War II began during Roosevelt's tenure, and Fala was made an honorary private in the army. He "contributed" a dollar every day for a year to show how he supported the war effort. In 1944, Fala joined FDR on a sea voyage to the Aleutian Islands. When Franklin campaigned for re-election, his opponents spread a rumor that the dog had been left on one of the islands, and that the president sent a ship to retrieve him at a cost of millions of taxpayer dollars. The terrier was buried near his master and was immortalized in a statue at the Roosevelt Memorial in D.C.—the only First Dog so honored.

"If you want a friend in Washington, get a dog" is a famous quote attributed to **Harry Truman**, who presided over the end of World War II and the beginning of the Cold War. No one is certain Truman actually said that—and if he did, he apparently didn't believe his own advice. When a supporter from his home state of Missouri gifted him with Feller, a cocker spaniel, Harry gave the dog away to his physician, which outraged the public. The pup was passed from one owner to another until it went to live on a farm. Though Truman didn't want dogs or other pets in the White House, he enjoyed feeding squirrels on the lawn—after all, they stayed outside.

Dwight David ("Ike") Eisenhower, a five-star general during World War II and Supreme Commander of the European Allied Forces, was also given a dog—Heidi, a Weimaraner, which was a relatively rare breed at the time. Unlike Truman, Ike was pleased with the gift—but after she had an accident on his expensive rug, she, too, was sent to a farm, where she lived happily. Eisenhower's other pet was a parakeet named Gabby, a favorite of his grandchildren. When Gabby died, she was laid to rest on the White House grounds. Ike's young grandson, David, visited the grave several times and reportedly thanked the gardener who buried the bird.

John F. Kennedy's daughter, Caroline, had a singing canary named Robin, which was also buried at the White House. She had a pony, Macaroni, as well, and the two were photographed for the cover of *Life* magazine. The photo is said to be the inspiration for Neil Diamond's song "Sweet Caroline." Another famous pet was Pushinka, daughter of Strelka, one of the Russian dogs that had gone to space aboard *Sputnik 2*. During JFK's term, relations with the Soviet Union were tense. But the leaders of both nations often exchanged presents, and the small dog was a gift from Soviet Premier Nikita Khrushchev. Khrushchev was reminding Kennedy that the Russians were winning the space race. JFK responded by declaring that America would soon put a man on the moon— and America did. However, some historians feel that Pushinka did help ease the tension and may even have prevented nuclear devastation. Although Kennedy was suspicious of the motive behind the gift, he and his family welcomed the dog. Pushinka had four puppies: Butterfly, White Tips, Blackie, and Streaker. Thousands of people asked to adopt the pups. Two children were chosen, and Butterfly and Streaker were sent to new homes. The other two dogs went to family friends. Their descendants may still be around today.

When **Lyndon Baines Johnson** picked up one of his beagles by the ears, he was barraged with angry letters, telegrams, and phone calls. Although he saw nothing wrong with the practice, he had to issue a public apology. In truth, LBJ loved his dogs and was often photographed with them. He owned several beagles, including Him and Her, and a white collie. However, his favorite dog was Yuki, a mixed breed that his daughter Luci found abandoned at a gas station in her father's hometown, Johnson City, Texas. Yuki attended Cabinet meetings, slept in the president's bed, and floated with him in the White House pool. But when LBJ wanted to include the dog in his daughter Lynda's wedding photo, his wife, Lady Bird, put her foot down. Johnson died in 1973 with Yuki by his side. His grandson wrote of his connection to the dog: "They shared a very significant bond that personified the American spirit: Only in America could a poor boy from Johnson City end up in the White House."

During **Richard Nixon**'s presidency, three dogs lived in the executive mansion—his Irish setter, King Timahoe; his daughter Julie's poodle, Vicki: and his other daughter Tricia's Yorkshire terrier, Pasha. But Nixon's best-known dog never lived in the White House at all. His name was Checkers, and he saved Nixon's political career. In 1952, when he was running for vice president, Nixon was accused of receiving secret donations. He went on television to deny the misuse of funds and said that there was one gift he would never return: the cocker spaniel his children adored. The address became known as the "Checkers speech." Though some saw the speech as melodramatic, it was a success. President Eisenhower and Vice President Nixon were swept into office.

After Nixon's political scandals, **Gerald Ford** wanted to heal the nation's wounds. For a pet, he chose one of the most popular service and therapy dog breeds in the U.S., the golden retriever. Liberty was a hit with the press and public, especially when she gave birth to nine puppies. The Fords kept one and named it Misty. In 1977, both Liberty and Misty and the other pups were featured on the Ford family Christmas card.

Jimmy Carter grew up on a farm surrounded by cows, pigs, ducks, horses, and dogs. But he had just two pets at the White House, both belonging to his daughter, Amy. Grits, a border collie mix, was given to Amy by her teacher, Verona Meeder. The dog was eventually returned to the teacher, possibly because Grits didn't get along with Amy's devoted cat, Misty Malarky Ying Yang. Misty had the distinction of lending his unique name to an instrumental by jazz guitarist Gabor Szabo.

Ronald Reagan brought no pets to Washington, D.C. During his second term in office, he received Lucky, a Bouvier des Flandres pup. The dog proved to be a handful, often dragging the president along by her leash, and she soon had to be sent to his ranch in California. Taking her place at the executive mansion was Rex, a Cavalier King Charles spaniel. Rex was also a leash puller, but smaller and easier to handle than Lucky. Some reporters claim that Reagan used the dog's escapades as an excuse to dodge their questions. Rex was frequently in the news. He had a tonsillectomy. He threw the switch to light the national Christmas tree. Then there were the reports of how the spaniel stood in the doorway of the supposedly haunted Lincoln bedroom, barked, and refused to enter. Whether or not Rex actually saw a ghost, it's true that the stories made good copy.

George H. W. Bush's springer spaniel, Millie, "wrote" a book about life in the White House. It was actually penned by First Lady Barbara Bush. Released in 1990, the book was a huge best seller. The Bushes donated all of the money they received from sales to a foundation for literacy, Barbara's major cause. During her stay at the executive mansion, Millie had pups. Her son, Ranger, is said to have been the president's favorite dog. Millie was also portrayed on several television shows, including *The Simpsons.* Bush mentioned the spaniel when he was campaigning for a second term as president against opponent Bill Clinton and his running mate, Al Gore: "My dog Millie knows more about foreign affairs than these two bozos." The public was not impressed, and Bush failed to be re-elected.

In 1991, a stray black-and-white cat adopted **Bill Clinton**'s daughter, Chelsea. Socks was quite a celebrity. He visited children at schools and hospitals. Featured in cartoons, comics, and TV shows, he even appeared as a Muppet on *Larry King Live,* where he was interviewed by guest host, Kermit the Frog. Six years later, the cat's solo status ended when he was joined by Buddy, the Clintons' enthusiastic new Labrador retriever. Socks hated Buddy immediately.

Like other presidents before him, **George W. Bush** had a presidency plagued with controversy. His pets provided a welcome respite. "Barney was by my side during our eight years in the White House. He never discussed politics and was always a faithful friend," he said about his Scottish terrier. For her birthday, George gave his wife, Laura, a second Scottie, which she named Miss Beazley, after a character in a children's book. He also owned one of Millie's pups—Spot, a springer spaniel.

When **Barack Obama** was running for office, he promised his two daughters that if he won, they would get a dog. He kept his word. Bo, a Portuguese water dog, was a gift from Senator Ted Kennedy, a fan of the breed. Bo has been the subject of many children's books. He was soon joined by Sunny, another Portie.

Donald Trump is one of the only presidents to have no pets. A spokesperson has said there are no plans at this time to add any. By contrast, Vice President Mike Pence has several, including Marlon Bundo, a rabbit featured in a book by his daughter Charlotte.

SELECTED BIBLIOGRAPHY/WEBOGRAPHY

Associated Press, "Lincoln to Thai King: Thanks but No Thanks for the Elephants," *New York Daily News,* March 24, 2018: http://www.nydailynews.com/newswires/news/world/lincoln -thai-king-thanks-no-thanks-elephants-article-1.3892995

Bologna, Caroline, "41 Photos of Presidential Pets Over Time," *HuffPost*, March 30, 2018: https://www.huffingtonpost.com/entry/41-photos-of-presidential-pets-over-time _us_5a8f2750e4b0664343557492

Borchard, Lauren, "A Presidential Cow," U.S. Capitol Historical Society, September 14, 2011: https://uschs.wordpress.com/2011/09/14/a-presidential-cow/

Bush, Barbara, *Millie's Book*, New York: Quill/William Morrow, 1990.

Coren, Stanley, "George Washington: President, General, and Dog Breeder," *Psychology Today*, January 2, 2009: https://www.psychologytoday.com/us/blog/canine-corner/200901/george -washington-president-general-and-dog-breeder

Coren, Stanley, *The Pawprints of History*, Free Press: New York, 2002.

Cox, Ana Marie, "Top Ten Presidential Pets in US History," *The Guardian*, August 20, 2013: https://www.theguardian.com/commentisfree/2013/aug/20/top-ten-presidential-pets

Gage, Joan, "Ronald Reagan's White House Ghost Story," *HuffPost*, October 31, 2013: https://www.huffingtonpost.com/joan-gage/white-house-ghosts_b_4175961.html

Gee, Alison, "Pushinka: A Cold War Puppy the Kennedys Loved," *BBC News*, January 6, 2014:
http://www.bbc.com/news/magazine-24837199

"Grant the Equestrian," *Ulysses S. Grant Homepage from the Keya Morgan Collection*:
http://www.granthomepage.com/grantequestrian.htm

Kelly, Kate, "LBJ's Dogs," *America Comes Alive!* https://americacomesalive.com/2011/07/28/lbjs
-dogs/

King, Gilbert, "The History of Pardoning Turkeys Began with Tad Lincoln," *Smithsonian.com*,
November 21, 2012: https://www.smithsonianmag.com/history/the-history-of-pardoning
-turkeys-began-with-tad-lincoln-141137570/

Kingson, Jennifer A., "Pomp, Circumstance, Fur: A Quiz on Presidential Pets," *The New York
Times*, September 30, 2016: https://www.nytimes.com/interactive/2016/09/30/us/politics
/00presidentialpetsquiz.html

Klein, Christopher, "The Thanksgiving Raccoon That Became a Presidential Pet," *History*,
November 18, 2016: https://www.history.com/news/the-thanksgiving-raccoon-that-became-a
-presidential-pet

Lang, Heather, "Lions and Tigers and Bears, Oh, My! Wild Animals at the White House," *The
National Children's Book and Literary Alliance*: http://ourwhitehouse.org/lions-and-tigers-and
-bear-oh-my-wild-animals-at-the-white-house/

Moberg, Julie, *Presidential Pets*, Watertown, Mass.: Imagine Books/Charlesbridge Publishing,
2012.

"Mockingbirds," *Thomas Jefferson Encyclopedia*: https://www.monticello.org/site/research-and
-collections/mockingbirds

"Our Capital's Finest Felines—A Look Back at Presidential Cats," *The Purring Post*, May, 2012:
http://www.purringpost.com/2012/05/15/our-capitals-finest-felines-a-look-back-at
-presidential-cats/

Pickens, Jennifer B., *Pets at the White House*, Dallas, Tex.: Fife & Drum Press, 2012. http://www.presidentialpetmuseum.com/

"Presidential Pets," CBS News: https://www.cbsnews.com/pictures/presidential-pets/

Reed, Margaret and Joan Lownds, *The Dogs of Camelot*, Guilford, Conn.: Lyons Press, 2018.

Resnick, Brian, "The Great White House Goat Chase," *The Atlantic*, May 29, 2015: https://www.theatlantic.com/politics/archive/2015/05/the-great-white-house-goat -chase/454449/

Resnick, Brian, "White House Sheep, A History," *The Atlantic*, October 17, 2014: https://www .theatlantic.com/politics/archive/2014/10/white-house-sheep-a-history/453405/

Rowan, Roy and Brooke Janis, *First Dogs*, Chapel Hill, N.C.: Algonquin Books of Chapel Hill, 2009.

Truman, Margaret, *White House Pets*, New York: David McKay Company, 1969.